Let's Meet
Ida B. Wells-Barnett

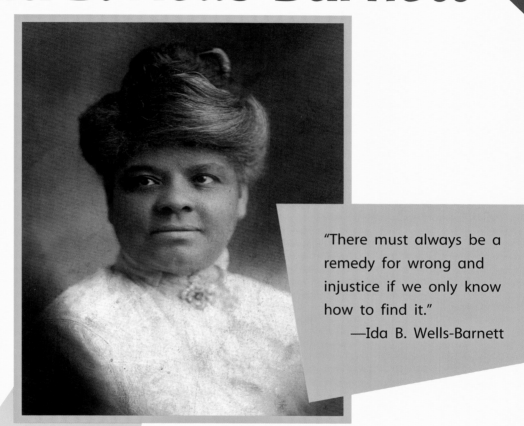

"There must always be a
remedy for wrong and
injustice if we only know
how to find it."
—Ida B. Wells-Barnett

Helen Frost

CHELSEA
CLUBHOUSE

An Imprint of Chelsea House Publishers
A Haights Cross Communications Company
Philadelphia

The Chelsea House World Wide Web address is www.chelseahouse.com

Printed and bound in the United States of America.

9 8 7 6 5 4 3 2 1

Library of Congress Cataloging-in-Publication Data
Frost, Helen, 1949–
    Let's meet Ida B. Wells-Barnett / Helen Frost.
        p. cm.—(Let's meet biographies)
Summary: Simple text and photographs introduce the life of Ida B. Wells-Barnett, a journalist who wrote about and spoke against the unfair treatment of African Americans.
Includes bibliographical references and index.
ISBN 0-7910-7320-3
1. Wells-Barnett, Ida B., 1862–1931—Juvenile literature. 2. African American women civil rights workers—Biography—Juvenile literature. 3. Civil rights workers—United States—Biography—Juvenile literature. 4. Journalists—United States—Biography—Juvenile literature. 5. African Americans—Civil rights—History—Juvenile literature. 6. Lynching—United States—History—Juvenile literature. 7. United States—Race relations—Juvenile literature. [1. Wells-Barnett, Ida B., 1862–1931. 2. Civil rights workers. 3. Journalists. 4. African Americans—Biography. 5. Women—Biography.] I. Title. II. Series.
E185.97.W55F76 2004
323'.092—dc21   2003004747

Editorial Credits

Lois Wallentine, editor; Takeshi Takahashi, designer; Mary Englar, photo researcher; Jennifer Krassy Peiler, layout

Content Reviewer

Donald Duster, grandson of Ida B. Wells

Photo Credits

University of Chicago Library Archives: cover, title page, 8, 10, 14, 18, 19, 21, 24; ©CORBIS: 4, 5, 9, 12, 17, 25, 26, 29; Memphis/Shelby County Public Library and Information Center: 6; Schomburg Center for Research in Black Culture, New York Public Library, Astor, Lenox and Tilden Foundations: 7, 11, 16, 27; ©Bettmann/CORBIS: 13, 20; University of Oklahoma Library: 15; Illinois State Historical Library: 22; Hulton Archive/Getty Images: 23.

Table of Contents

Growing Up

Ida Bell Wells was born into **slavery** on July 16, 1862. Her parents were James and Elizabeth. Most slaves in the South worked in the fields. But James learned to be a **carpenter**. His master sent him to work for a man named Bolling, who was a builder. Elizabeth was a cook for Bolling.

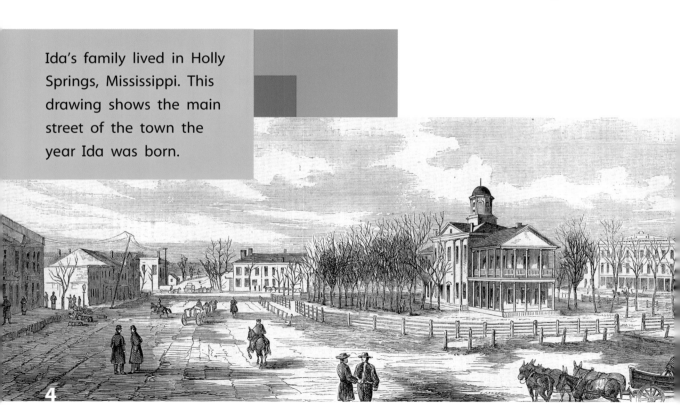

Ida's family lived in Holly Springs, Mississippi. This drawing shows the main street of the town the year Ida was born.

Both adults and children went to schools set up for newly freed slaves. Ida's mother went to school with her children, so she could learn to read the Bible.

Ida was born during the **Civil War**. In 1865, the war ended, and slaves were freed. At first, James worked for Bolling as a paid **employee**. Later, he opened his own carpentry business.

Ida soon had six brothers and sisters. "Our job was to go to school and learn all we could," Ida later wrote.

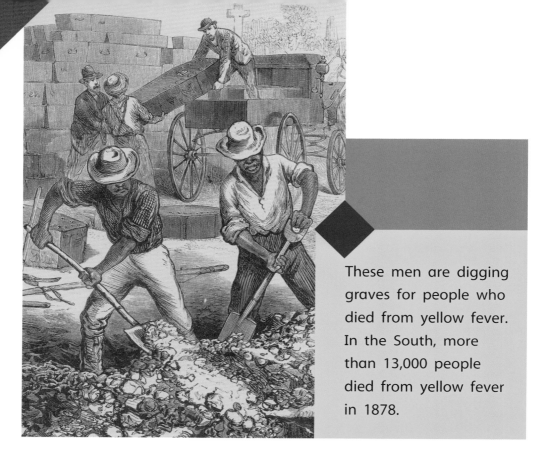

These men are digging graves for people who died from yellow fever. In the South, more than 13,000 people died from yellow fever in 1878.

In 1878, Ida's parents and baby brother died of **yellow fever**. Friends wanted to take care of the children. But they would have to live in separate homes. Sixteen-year-old Ida told them that the family was not going to split up. She found a job as a teacher in order to keep her family together.

That first year, Ida's grandmother or a friend stayed with the children during the week. Ida taught in a country school near Holly Springs. She stayed with students' families on weeknights. For the weekends, Ida rode a mule back to town. She did the cleaning and cooking for her family while she was home.

Ida may have taught in a schoolroom like this one.

Ida enjoyed living in Memphis. She took college classes and joined a group of teachers who met weekly to read poetry and articles from a paper called *Evening Star*.

Ida knew she could earn more money for the family in a larger city. But her family would have to split up. In 1879, Ida and two of her sisters moved in with their aunt in Memphis, Tennessee. Ida's other sister and two brothers stayed with another aunt on a farm near Holly Springs.

Ida found a teaching job near Memphis. She rode the train back and forth from her job to the city.

On May 4, 1884, Ida was riding in the first-class train car, as she usually did. She had a ticket for this car, but the conductor told her to move to a car for smokers. He said first-class was only for white people.

Ida would not move. When the conductor tried to make Ida move, she bit him. Two men helped pull Ida out of the car and off the train.

A conductor tells a black man to move to a different train car. In the late 1800s, railroad companies made rules that said blacks could no longer ride in first-class cars with white people.

suit for my peo[ple]
have firmly belie[ved]
that the law was [...]
and would, when [...]
it, give us justice.
of that belief and [...]
aged, and just now
possible would gather my ra[ce]
in my arms and fly far a-
way with them. O God is there
no redress, no peace, no justice
in this land for us? Thou hast
always fought the battles of the
weak & oppressed. Come to my
aid at this moment & teach me
what to do, for I am sorely, bit
-terly disappointed. Show us the

Ida wrote in her diary about losing the court case. She asked, "Is there no redress, no peace, no justice in this land for us?"

Ida hired a lawyer and pressed charges against the railroad. She won. The judge told the railroad to pay her $500.

Later, a higher court overturned the case. Ida had to pay $200 in court costs. Ida wrote in her diary that she felt discouraged. She wanted to "gather my race in my arms and fly far away with them."

Ida started writing articles for a few newsletters. She realized that she enjoyed writing more than teaching. In 1889, she became a part owner of a Memphis newspaper called *Free Speech and Headlight*. She soon quit teaching and became a full-time **journalist**.

Ida became angry when she heard about people being treated unfairly. She used her articles to **protest** wrongdoing.

Ida signed her articles with the name "Iola." She became well-known as someone who spoke her mind and told the truth.

Writing about Racism

Even though slavery ended in 1865, **racism** still made life hard for blacks. Many white people thought they were better than black people. Some states and cities passed laws to keep blacks and whites separate. Under those laws, blacks had to use separate restrooms, drinking fountains, and waiting rooms. Laws in some states kept black people from voting. Ida wrote articles about how racism hurt black people.

Well into the 1900s, many cities still had separate schools for black children and white children. Ida once wrote about how schools for white students in Memphis were better than schools for blacks.

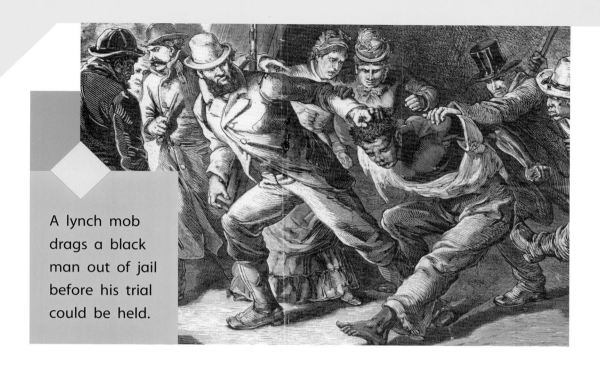

A lynch mob drags a black man out of jail before his trial could be held.

Black people often were not treated fairly under the law. White people could charge a black person with a crime, even though there was little proof. The police would put the black person in jail to wait for a **trial**.

But sometimes an angry mob would gather before a trial could be held. They would pull the black person out of jail and shoot or hang the person. This act was called **lynching**.

Ida's friend, Thomas Moss, became a **victim** of lynching. He and two friends owned a grocery store in Memphis. Many black people shopped at their store instead of a nearby store owned by a white man. In March 1892, a group of white people attacked Thomas's store. During the fight, white men were wounded. The police put Thomas and his friends in jail. But before a trial could be held, a lynch mob killed them.

Ida (left) is pictured here with Thomas Moss's wife, Betty, and their children.

Ida wrote that black people should "leave a town which will neither protect our lives and property, nor give us a fair trial in the courts." She encouraged blacks to move to Oklahoma, as this family did.

Before he died, Thomas said, "Tell my people to go West—there is no justice for them here." Ida carried out her friend's wish. She wrote an article telling black people in Memphis to move West. Ida also asked blacks who stayed to stop riding streetcars and shopping at white-owned stores.

Many blacks did as Ida suggested. Within two months, 6,000 black people moved West. Many white business owners lost their black customers.

SOUTHERN HORRORS.
LYNCH LAW
IN ALL
ITS PHASES

Miss IDA B. WELLS.

Price, - - - Fifteen Cents.

THE NEW YORK AGE PRINT.
1892.

Ida wrote this booklet to bring attention to the problem of lynching.

Ida started **investigating** lynching cases. Many black men had been charged with attacking white women. Ida talked to the men's family members and to the white women. Ida found out that the women hadn't been attacked after all.

Ida wrote articles and booklets about lynching. She included facts that proved the innocence of many lynching victims. She also gave speeches about lynching in northern U.S. cities and in England.

Many white people did not like Ida's articles. In May 1892, a group of white men destroyed her newspaper office. They said they would kill Ida if she came back to Memphis.

Ida was in New York City at the time. She knew she couldn't go back. She took a job with the *New York Age*. This newspaper helped Ida continue her protest against lynching.

After Ida spoke in England, many British people held protests against lynching crimes in the United States. These protests put pressure on the U.S. government to do something about the problem.

Making a Difference

Ferdinand Barnett was a lawyer as well as a newspaper owner and editor. He sold the newspaper to Ida before they were married.

In 1893, Ida decided to move to Chicago, Illinois. She took a job with the *Chicago Conservator*. Ferdinand L. Barnett owned and edited this newspaper.

Like Ida, Ferdinand believed in working for civil rights for blacks. He and Ida fell in love. They were married on June 27, 1895. After Ida married, her name was Ida B. Wells-Barnett.

Ida kept writing and giving speeches. But after her second child was born, she didn't travel as much as she had before. In Chicago, Ida formed a women's club to support needs in the community. One of its projects was to open a kindergarten for both white and black children in a local church.

Ida's Family

Ida and Ferdinand had four children. Ida expected her children to work hard in school and earn good grades.

Ida

Herman

Charles

Alfreda

Ida "Jr."

In 1898, a black postmaster was lynched in South Carolina. Ida traveled to Washington, D.C., and told President William McKinley about the lynching. He told Ida he would look into the case, but nothing happened. Ida was disappointed.

Ida thought President William McKinley would take action against lynching when a black postmaster, who was a government employee, was lynched. McKinley did not help.

In 1909, Ida didn't want to get involved in investigating another lynching. But her son Charles said, "Mother if you don't go nobody else will."

Anger grew between blacks and whites, even in northern states. **Riots** broke out in several cities. Mobs burned homes and stores owned by blacks. In 1909, a lynch mob killed a black man in Cairo, Illinois. Ida heard that the sheriff, Frank Davis, had let it happen. She knew there was a law that a sheriff had to try to stop a lynching.

Ida traveled to Cairo and talked to people who knew about the case. Then she went to Springfield, Illinois, where Sheriff Davis was on trial. Ida spoke at the trial, giving the facts against Davis. Governor Charles Deneen listened to Ida. He fired Sheriff Davis. The governor also said he would provide state troops to help local police officers fight lynch mobs. No more lynchings happened in Illinois.

Governor Charles Deneen decided that a sheriff who failed to protect a prisoner from a lynch mob should lose his job. He worked to stop all lynchings in the state.

In 1917, the NAACP organized a parade to protest against lynching. People marched to the sound of drumbeats.

In 1909, Ida joined a group of black and white leaders who formed the **National Association for the Advancement of Colored People (NAACP)**. Ida spoke to the group about lynching. She wanted them to ask the government to make lynching a crime, but members could not agree on a statement. It took several years before the NAACP started to speak out against lynching.

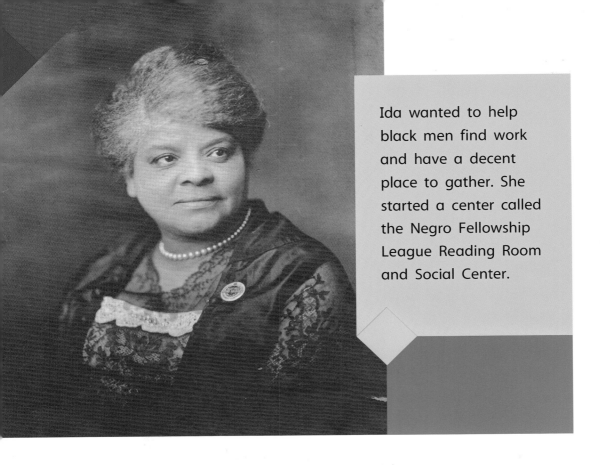

Ida wanted to help black men find work and have a decent place to gather. She started a center called the Negro Fellowship League Reading Room and Social Center.

Ida continued to help blacks in Chicago. She wanted to make a place where black men could gather. In 1910, she started a center for black men and boys. Visitors could read, talk with others, and search for a job. They could pay 15 cents for a bed at night. Ida kept the center open for 10 years.

In the early 1900s, women were protesting for the right to vote. Ida founded a club for black women. Members of her club marched with white women in a voting rights parade in Chicago.

In 1919, women's rights leaders organized a national parade in Washington, D.C. Leaders told Ida that they were afraid that Southern women wouldn't want to march with black women. Ida went and marched with the women from Illinois.

On March 3, 1919, about 8,000 women marched in Washington, D.C. for the right to vote.

Ida's Honors

Ida saw women win the right to vote in 1920. By the 1930s, lynching was no longer common. Ida's work had made life better for black Americans and for women. Ida died on March 25, 1931, when she was 68 years old.

Ida was honored many times after her death. In 1941, city officials named a large housing project the Ida B. Wells Homes. In 1950, Ida was named an outstanding woman in Chicago history.

This photograph of the Ida B. Wells housing project was taken in 1942.

Ida is known today as an early leader of the civil rights movement.

Some people call Ida the mother of the **civil rights movement**. She stood up for what was right. She used her articles and speeches to call others to action. Through her protests, she helped others see that it is possible to change unfair rules and to seek fair treatment for everyone.

Important Dates in Ida's Life

1862   Ida is born on July 16 in Holly Springs, Mississippi.

 Age 16   1878   Ida's parents and brother die of yellow fever; Ida becomes a teacher to support the family.

1879   Ida's aunts each take three of the children; Ida lives with her aunt in Memphis and teaches in Shelby County.

 Age 22   1884   Ida wins a lawsuit against the Chesapeake, Ohio, and Southwestern Railway Company; a higher court later reverses the decision.

1889   Ida becomes part owner and writer for the *Free Speech and Headlight* newspaper.

 Age 29   1892   A lynch mob kills Thomas Moss, Calvin McDowell, and Henry Stewart; Ida begins her anti-lynching efforts; Ida moves to New York City after her newspaper office is destroyed.

1893   Ida takes a job with the *Chicago Conservator*.

 Age 33   1895   Ida marries Ferdinand Barnett.

1898   Ida meets President William McKinley to discuss anti-lynching laws.

 Age 47   1909   Ida gains the support of Illinois Governor Charles Deneen to stop lynching in the state; Ida helps to start the NAACP.

1910   Ida opens a shelter and gathering place for men and boys in Chicago.

1913   Ida starts the Alpha Suffrage Club for black women.

1919   Ida marches in a voting rights parade in Washington, D.C.

1931   Ida dies on March 25 in Chicago.

 Age 63   1941   The city of Chicago names a housing project after Ida.

1950   Ida is named an outstanding woman in Chicago history.

More about the Black Press

Launched in New York City in 1827, *Freedom's Journal* became the first newspaper to be owned and operated by black people. Before this time, articles about blacks were seldom printed in white-owned newspapers. *Freedom's Journal* was the first to give black people their own voice.

This photograph from the early 1900s shows reporters, editors, and typesetters working on an issue of the *Virginia Baptist Newspaper*, a black-owned business in Richmond, Virginia.

Another 40 black-owned newspapers began publishing in northern cities before the Civil War. Papers like *North Star*, owned by Frederick Douglass, reported on movements to end slavery in the South. The papers offered a means of uniting the black community behind the effort.

Ida B. Wells-Barnett worked for black-owned newspapers in Memphis, New York City, and Chicago. It was one way she could speak to many people of her own race. She spoke out against injustice.

From the end of the Civil War until the early 1900s, many black journalists wrote articles telling black people in the South to move North. Black-owned newspapers also gave information to help those who had moved find jobs and homes. But people soon saw that racism caused problems in the North as well as in the South. Black journalists wrote about those problems.

By the 1920s, there were more than 500 black-owned newspapers in the United States. These papers supported the struggle for civil rights and became an important vehicle for political movements that helped blacks.

Today, black journalists write for all major newspapers.

Glossary

carpenter—a person who builds things out of wood, such as houses or furniture

civil rights movement—In the United States, African Americans and people of different backgrounds had to struggle to have their legal rights recognized; some civil rights in the United States are the right to own property, the right to equal treatment under the law, and the right to vote.

Civil War—the U.S. war between the North and the South that lasted from 1861 to 1865; resulted in slaves being freed.

employee—a person who works for and is paid by another person or business

investigate—to find out as much as possible about something; Ida talked to people, read articles in white owned papers, and looked at police reports to investigate lynching cases.

journalist—someone who collects information and writes articles for newspapers, magazines, television, or radio

lynching—killing someone without a trial; lynching is often carried out by a mob.

National Association for the Advancement of Colored People (NAACP)—an organization founded in 1909 by a group of black and white leaders to work for fair treatment and opportunities for black people

protest—to say or to show you are against something

racism—the belief that one race, or group of people with the same physical features (such as skin color), is better than other races; people who are racist treat members of other races unfairly or cruelly.

riot—the actions of a noisy, angry group of people; during a riot, people may fight each other, damage property, and burn buildings.

slavery—the practice of forcing people to work without pay

trial—a meeting held in a court of law to examine the facts of a case and decide if a charge against a person is true or false

victim—a person who is hurt, killed, or made to suffer

yellow fever—a disease that can cause death; it spreads through mosquito bites.

To Learn More

▶ **Read these books:**

Medearis, Angela Shelf. *Princess of the Press: The Story of Ida B. Wells-Barnett*. New York: Lodestar Books, 1997.

McKissack, Patricia and Fredrick McKissack. *Ida B. Wells-Barnett: A Voice Against Violence*. Great African-Americans. Berkeley Heights, NJ: Enslow, 2001.

Pinkney, Andrea Davis. *Let It Shine: Stories of Black Women Freedom Fighters*. San Diego: Gulliver Books, Harcourt, Inc., 2000.

▶ **Look up these Web sites:**

Black History Month — Biography — Ida B. Wells-Barnett

http://www.galegroup.com/free_resources/bhm/bio/wells_i.htm
   Read a short biography about Ida. Click on "Biographies" to link to articles about other figures in black history.

The Black Press Archives

http://www.blackpressusa.com/history/archive_essay.asp?NewsID=257&Week=12
   Learn more about Ida's work by reading the article that appeared in the Chicago Defender *newspaper after her death in 1931.*

The Black Press: Soldiers Without Swords

http://www.pbs.org/blackpress/film/index.html
   Find out about the rise of black-owned newspapers in the United States and their role in shaping history.

Ida B. Wells Museum

http://www.idabwells.org
   Visit a museum in Holly Springs, Mississippi, that is named after Ida and located in the house in which she was born.

We Shall Overcome—Ida B. Wells Barnett House

http://www.cr.nps.gov/nr/travel/civilrights/il2.htm
   View photograph of the house in Chicago where Ida and Ferdinand lived from 1919–1929 and review another article about Ida.

Index